Your A.H.A. Moment Begins Now
By Archbishop Harpazio Anastasis

Manifesting any idea supposedly takes great devotion; even greater devotion to grow from success toward wealth.

With this in mind it was deemed necessary (by the world's most material world resistant person), that a System of Teaching (Catechism) should be erected, in order to assist the convergence of the spiritual (ideal) state of any idea to that of logical material manifestation.

This dire need was all due to epic failures - at obtaining clarity of execution - for the beginning, middle, and end of Great Ideas, by the writer of this book, **A**rchbishop **H**arpazio **A**nastasis.

If a System of Teaching could both inspire and motivate the Bishop to pursue his own dreams and make them a reality, then surely it could help other people, who (like him) have struggled their whole life with a mind that resembles storm clouds of rebellious unharnessed thoughts!

Do you have a billion ideas running around through your brain?

If so, then you could truly benefit from a <u>brain focus discovery</u> that trains your thoughts to become obedient enough, to determine which ones are worthy of your most precious attention.

The desires you have which are willing to become subservient to <u>the invention discovered by The Bishop</u>, are the noble ones you will want to adopt into your Kingdom of Entrepreneurship.

These words you are now reading are not meant to draw your attention to The Bishop, but rather exalt you to the <u>triumphant colorful image</u> you see at the beginning of this book; the evidence of a true A.H.A Moment™ that occurred for him, and could occur for you.

Firstly, know that Archbishop Harpazio Anastasis (henceforth referenced as A.H.A.) sends you forth as an Apostle, Prophet, Evangelist, and Pastor of your Great Idea/s.

The image above contains 12 colors which are truly a reflection of the 12 Issues of Entrepreneurship™, a 13th issue being the Conscious Strategy that clearly relates all 12 issues one to another.

Secondly, A.H.A. reveals to you the significance of accepting yourself as an Apostle, Prophet, Evangelist, and Pastor of your Great Idea:

Apostle   Prophet   Evangelist   Pastor

Your Mission   Your Motive   Your Impact   Your Legacy

Therefore, when you have called out and assembled any group of people, small or great, to the realization of your idea, you have created a Church that is influenced by your Mission, Motive, Impact, and Legacy.

You should know that Merlin and Bishop are both titles that have practically the same meanings, and you could become the Archbishop of your Great Idea/s.

Merlin means "Seer to the king" and Bishop means "Overseer".
Merlin was never one person, but there was one Merlin whom we all love and adore: the Seer who magically stuck the Excalibur Sword into the stone.

In the same way that Merlin of old supervised the success of Sir Arthur - to manifest and fortify Camelot- the Arch-Bishop/Arch-Merlin who writes this short book for your inspiration and innovation also does elevate you to his mystical teachings.

These are all secretly contained in the aforementioned IMAGE called **The Square X Factor**™ .

You've likely heard of the *X Factor*?

It is the concept that someone "has what it takes" to succeed.

Factors can be both nouns and verbs.

www.dictionary.com says this of the word, "Factor":

<u>As a Noun</u>
"One of the elements contributing to a particular result or situation."

"One of two or more numbers, algebraic expressions, or the like, that when multiplied together produce a given product."

<u>As A Verb</u>
"Factor in/into – to include as an essential element, especially in forecasting or planning."

The Square X Factor™ image and meaning contains every essential factor, that when multiplied together, cause your **Great Idea** to manifest success, gain, and wealth.

And for your dearest and most relevant consideration, know that you could immediately seize or be caught up by force (rapture/harpazio) - by the words being written right before your eyes - into instant success (clearly defined very soon as you read further).

Your Merlin Wand   Your Avalon Cup   Your Excalibur Sword   Your Camelot Coin

Through your Merlin Wand (Apostolic Mission) you Create your Idea, through your Avalon Cup (Prophetic Motive) you Preserve your idea, through your Excalibur Sword (Evangelistic Impact) you Destroy and Innovate your Idea, and through Your Camelot Coin (Pastoral Legacy) you set your Idea Free.

Your A.H.A. Moment™ is awakening within you now and you can perceive **The Square X Factor**™ .

There are 4 major success, gain, and wealth Apostles, Prophets, Evangelists, and Pastors of our Age of time...

...They are Andrew Carnegie (Symbolic of the Bishop's Mission), Napoleon Hill (Symbolic of the Bishop's Motives), Earl Nightingale (Symbolic of the Bishop's Impact), and Bob Proctor (Symbolic of the Bishop's Legacy).

In his book "The Gospel of Wealth" Andrew Carnegie - founder of Carnegie Hall - enflamed the world's potential desire for wealth, by proclaiming a spiritual-material mission.

Carnegie's Spiritual Ideology defended the rich and the poor, but also attempted to philosophically bridge the gap between the two by revealing the key differences in mission, motive, impact, and legacy.

Essentially, it is the opinion of Archbishop Harpazio Anastasis that the great majorities of the poor are weak in mission, dishonest in their motives, have little sense of their impact on society, and are born victim to no sense of being able to pass on any kind of appreciable inheritance to their offspring.

Therefore - by default - you having a Great Idea you intend to manifest is an automatic indication that you have intended to arise out of poverty's aimless, deceitful, irresponsible, and inheritance void state of existence.

Andrew Carnegie selected a student by the name of Napoleon Hill to scientifically observe hundreds of people whose outward appearance showed evidence of being wealthy.

Mr. Hill's primary unique revelation was that all of these people had realized the role and power of their subconscious, for manifesting or preventing ideas.

But then a great radio broadcaster named Earl Nightingale arose as a student of Napoleon Hill and brought an impactful message; he said, "Success is the progressive revelation of a worthy ideal."

Mr. Nightingale defined a worthy ideal as, "A nonconformist ideal", one that any person has "predetermined" they are going to manifest.

And finally, the contemporary Bob Proctor decided to apply Mr. Hill's and Mr. Nightingale's teachings to the best of his ability, and he established a Legacy for future generations called, "The Proctor-Gallagher Institute".

What has been gifted to society with extravagant teaching are 4 Great Freedoms of Thought, Emotion, Speech, and Action; embodied in the 4 Great Humanitarians mentioned.

They are the pioneering predecessors of what could only be rightfully called **The Materialist School of Science**.

But their scientific methods are best understood in the context of "authentic human interaction", that of humans experimenting with each other's innovations /intuitions, and to multiply the possibility for ideas to manifest clearly/speedily; popularly referred to as "Master-mind Alliances."

Nevertheless, in recent years many attempted to form a master-mind alliance and produced a movie called, "The Law of Attraction".

It claimed that we manifest what we think, that "thinking about" certain things will cause them to come to pass; and this imbalanced claim created myriads of cotton candy in the sky philosophies.

There developed an "imbalance in the force" so to speak – because of the Law of Attraction film.

The imbalance in the force caused a great amount of humanity (who had eaten the cotton candy of the movie) to experience a deep and great sense of disappointment; knowing that despite all the time and effort they spent "thinking about" their ideas, what they had eaten disappeared quite quickly in their information eating mouths.

But such great disappointments also assist to create a more fervent passionate hunger for the bridging of the seeming enormous gap between spirituality (idealism) and materiality (idea manifestation).

And it is from both the deep cravings for true solutions and the acceptance of true solutions that your A.H.A. Moment™ will occur for yourself and for society.

What has been desperately needed by the world is the resurgence and discovery of listening to Andrew Carnegie's message - his Good News of Wealth; but with contemporary terminology and innovative explanation.

Mr. Carnegie preached a practical scientific method of bridging the gap between the rich (those who demonstrate the ability to manifest their ideas) and the poor (those who demonstrate an inability to manifest their ideas).

The bridging of the rich/poor gap should have no bell ring of cotton candy in the sky.

Instead, the bridge should be such a precipice to walk across that both the wealthy and the poverty stricken feel like they can easily journey to each other's "sides", without feeling like they are at odds with each other.

With all that in mind, you should know that this book is not meant to touch on what Carnegie wrote regarding the ethics of becoming wealthy or the follies or remaining poor.

Rather, this book is meant to touch on the crystal clear proof that **The Square X Factor**™ _image and meanings_ present _a very practical way to immediately_ apply Carnegie's teachings and become _successful_:

<u>Realizing a progressive revelation of your Worthy Ideal</u>

And by success, A.H.A. does not necessary mean wealth; as matter of fact, the benefits of embracing his <u>System of Teaching</u> (known elsewhere in other writings as <u>Katechism</u>™) include acquiring <u>a very clear distinction between Success, Gain and Wealth</u>.

**"You're A.H.A. Moment" deals strictly with how to become successful, the claim being that the immediate success you could achieve (by reading this book) is a sure foundation for the profitability of business ownership and your wealth enterprise ventures.**

With all that in mind revisit all the images above and their meanings before looking at the deeper correspondences below, **so you can experience success BEFORE** you take on business ownership or enterprise risks.

The 4 Magical Weapons of Success
(Allows you to immediately realize your worthy ideal)

Merlin Wand	Avalon Cup	Excalibur Sword	Camelot Coin
Freedom of Thought	Freedom of Emotion	Freedom of Speech	Freedom of Action
Mission	Motive	Impact	Legacy
Spirituality	Psychology	Intellectualism	Materialism
Fiery Idealism	Watery Emotionalism	Airy Speech	Earthy Action
Creation	Preservation	Destructive/Constructive	Redemptive
Futuristic	Past	Present	Timeless
Apostolic	Prophetic	Evangelistic	Pastoral
Andrew Carnegie	Napoleon Hill	Earl Nightingale	Bob Proctor

You may wonder why "The Past" and "Prophetic" are categorized as such, since that prophesy is often associated with the future?

It is because the future actions and words we choose to do and say are deeply rooted in what is instilled in our sub-conscious.

Therefore a true prophet is someone who can identify an Emotional Root, and determine not only where it is planted but what kind of seed it sprang from.

When you gather yourself together (ie. become a church) with other human beings who are also conscious of the many correspondences defining **The 4 Magical Weapons of Success™**, you also join yourself with the 4 aforementioned legendary human archetypes of history, who paved the way for the success, gain, and wealth of your Great Idea/s.

<u>Let us walk the path together, which has already been cleared</u>.

You have read, "Archbishop Harpazio Anastasis", but may have been asking yourself, "Archbishop of what?"

An Archbishop claims Bishopric (supervisor role) over a church - a community of people.

A.H.A. claims Bishopric – Merlin Status - of a Church, a modern day Camelot that heralds the rise of a legendary allegorical King Arthur:

<u>YOU</u>

Through *Intellectual Assessment* you will pull your Excalibur from the Stone (the illusion that your material world circumstances are preventing the manifestation of your Great Ideas).

The Square X Factor™ can be embraced at every phase of dissection, externally or internally, with complete intellectual authenticity.

Somehow, for an apparent unknown and bizarre reason, Merlin - your Merlin who writes this short book - has been gifted with the ability to transform over 14 years of esoteric study, into practical and material world realizations that defy reason and also fully exalt logic.

The word logic comes from the Greek word, "Logos" which means, "a reasoned out thought."

<u>When you look at the simplicity of **The Square X Factor**™ image, you see reason at every turn.</u>

But the Logo/Logos imparted to you through this writing is from the simplicity of silence; about 3 to 4 months' worth of meditation, experimentation, and artistry; so that there evolved complete congruence of meaning.

<u>Success was achieved; a progressive revelation of his worthy ideal.</u>

In late 2014, A.H.A. realized his worthy ideal to carry on Andrew Carnegie's Mission to bridge the gap between the rich and poor, by creating a System of Teaching that Knights anyone – anywhere - worthy of success, gain, and wealth.

And what happens when you are knighted by **The Royal Content Family**™ *whose* <u>**family crest**</u> *is the SEAL of the IMAGE of* **The Square X Factor**™?

You embark on a Quest for the Holy Grail, that is, the unveiling of your Subconscious in 3 Categories of Emotion:

1. The Story of Your Idea's Manifestation

2. The Company Culture (principles that drive your motivation)

3. The Transformational Needs of Yourself and Prospects (knowledge, money, things, anything you are emotionally attached to that needs transformation)

But Psychological Freedom is only 25% of the 4-Fold Revelation of Success – Your Worthy Ideal.

Historically, it is rumored that Merlin (seer to the king) took on many roles in society, as was customary for Druids.

At that time Roman Catholicism was being established as a universal religion for the world to embrace.

Somehow Merlin maneuvered himself into the role of Roman Catholic Priest.

Close examination of Druidic history reveals a paradox that this mystical head of the revered "Oak Men" society embraced teachings completely contradictory to the Druid belief system.

Was his role play merely political in nature?

To help answer this question A.H.A. has a work of historical fiction in mind called, "Dark Merlin: Founder of Roman Catholicism".

But more important to this day and age, a real modern idea manifestation community exists called **Metatron Church**^{TM}, comprised of those who embrace – even superficially – the teachings of **The Square X Factor**^{TM}.

Parishioners (sojourners) are offered an opportunity to baptize themselves with Success, Gain, and Wealth through a contemporary model of dependence (success), independence (gain), and interdependence (wealth).

Parishioners are introduced to **The 12 Issues of Entrepreneurship**^{TM} (the 12 colors in the Logo/Logos), and are provided a strategy for using the awareness of those issues for their own advantage.

Your act of reading this book and accepting the truths contained herein for yourself immediately grants you status as a parishioner- sojourner - in our midst.

It is no withheld secret that The 12 Issues of Entrepreneurship^{TM} are intrepidly based on Astrology's ancient 12 Houses (Constellations), which your Merlin has proprietarily called The 12 Issues of Life^{TM}.

The ancient astronomical-astrological claim is that every human being is born under a Rising (Ascendant) Sign at the time of their birth.

Since the earth rotates through a different Zodiac Mark every 2 hours, then it is philosophically claimed by astrologers that whatever a person's sign is, represents how the "world perceives you".

In this regard the Rising Sign is viewed as an Astrological Mask, because <u>how the world perceives us is not necessarily our "true self"</u>, but supposedly our Sun Signs represent our True Self.

At the age of 20, in the year 2000, your Archbishop had embarked on a spiritual quest wholly unmotivated by material world benefits (no material profit considered).

This journey led him to buy the book, "The Rising Sign" by Jeanne Avery.

Being forced by sheer study and personal experience confirmation, to take Astrology's Rising Sign 12 Issues of Life™ seriously, he also sought relevancy for individuals to become aware of this knowledge.

Firstly, he received a sense of peace about how the world perceived him growing up, and he was certain that anyone else could benefit from the assurances that the way they had always been interacting with the world is not an accident.

He took great comfort knowing that Howard Hughes and Walt Disney both shared his same Virgo Rising Sign, suffering both the same problems and enjoying the same benefits.

The relatability of being able to compare oneself with historical and celebrity figures mentioned in Jeanne Avery's book brought him a great sense of equilibrium with the rest of humanity.

Secondly, prior to reading The Rising Sign, your Archbishop was already on a mission to help individuals experience their "true identity".

Yet he knew this would not be possibly unless first experiencing his own false identity on all levels: spiritually, emotionally, intellectually, and materially.

And there even eventually came a time when he actually felt he'd discovered "the Holy Grail of Spirituality".

Yet his conclusion was that even if his discoveries were true, it did neither him, nor the rest of the world any real good, if these treasures were given without practical significance.

Of course his attention and care, regarding the relevancy of all the esoteric "revelations", is itself operating proof of his Virgo Rising Sign, which naturally places priority to practicality and research over blind acceptance or "the wow factor".

But even though through the many years since the beginning of "The Quest", he had considered producing material which emphasized intellectual proof of spirituality, he also determined that even intellectual proof is not good enough to serve the light speed needs of the Internet Generation.

The craving of humanity is not just for Intellectual Scholarship of Ideal Truths of Metaphysical claims, but for everything which has been deemed Metaphysical to have some sort of Material Significance that can <u>actually help</u> Individuals within the Global Society to evolve materially, in a manner which benefits current and future generations.

In early 2014 the phrase "authentic human interaction" became a resounding theme for your Archbishop, because he had been burnt out by spam floods in his Twitter account.

Also, Facebook posts screamed in Facebook Groups and on his regular Facebook profile page, "Look at me! Look at me!", in addition to other forms of assault through unauthentic interactions.

He intensely desired a way for people to connect with each other through a hybrid offline and offline approach that could drastically help to improve the ecosystem of social media interaction on the Internet.

And with much frustration and sincere thoughts toward a solution, the A.H.A Moment™ came in November of 2014 - Archbishop Harpazio Anastasis was officially conceived.

In the middle of watching the pilot for the brand new hit TV Show on the CW called, "The Flash"...in a flash...A.H.A. realized that we all have the potential to become Meta-human, through the instant light communication of the Internet.

Why is that significant to anyone seeking to manifest their ideas?

Because this discovery is not sourced from Metaphysical "cotton candy in the sky" preaching that is often spouted off by "this" guru and "that" guru.

This is something entirely fresh; a complete view of evolved humanity in the Age of the Internet.

And this draws us near to the meaning of the Greek word "Meta".

Today it has evolved to mean "about".

For example, the identity, "Metatron Church: The Religion of Business" implies that the Church is a Religion about Business.

But it is also a "business about business".

While all that is very true, the name is inspired from the original meaning of **Meta**:

Beyond/after

The true A.H.A Moment™ came to Merlin Harpazio Anastasis by researching the purity of the Greek language and dissecting the real implied meaning of Meta.

His even greater epiphany came when he inadvertently looked up the Greek word for repentance: *Meta-naos* .

Having grown up involved with the descendant religions of Roman Catholicism, such as Protestantism and Pentecostalism, your Merlin discovered how these organizations developed their notion of "guilt and remorse".

They were interpreting the word through the modern lens of Meta, meaning "about".

Naos means "to think".

So when the concept "repent of your sins" is interpreted as "to think" "about" sin, an entire inaccurate paradigm is born.

But that is not what the pre-Roman Government "Christians" were admonished to do.

For them repentance meant "to think beyond" the sin.

And what is the Greek meaning of sin?

It means "to miss the mark/to lack/to be without", much like the Spanish word "sin" literally means "without".

If you have a bow, arrow, and a target and miss the mark it means one of 4 things:

1) Your bow is not good enough
2) Your arrow is not good enough
3) Your pull and aim is not good enough
4) Your skill is not good enough

No matter what "lacks", repentance essentially means you "think beyond the failure".

Your passion to hit the mark must be greater than the fact that you missed the mark!

It will likely ruffle the feathers of some readers to be forced to admit that no matter what you think sin or failure is in your life, there was *NEVER EVER* any factual teachings from the founder of Christendom nor his Apostles (sent out ones) that indicates any person is supposed to focus on their failures!

<u>Here is your practical lesson of all these discoveries for your immediate benefit</u>:

- You have an idea you want manifest (the mark)
- You craft a Bow (Your Passion)
- You craft an Arrow (Your Identity)
- You identify how your audience relates to your Mark (Marketing)
- You Release your Arrow (Identity) through your Passion (the pull of the string and steady concentration) at your Target (Marketing)

So how are passion, identity, and marketing related?

They all represent <u>Categories</u> of Thought: Metadata.

Metadata could simply be "data about data".

But the Metadata referenced in the Metatron Church^{TM} community is "Data beyond the Data".

<u>Whenever you create a Website you are infusing the data that is in your innermost thoughts into the World of the Internet - **Metahuman** reality - the reality beyond the human.</u>

Yet we have discovered through Social Media that there is an oneness between the Meta and the Human!

SPAM is the antithesis to the Authentic Human Interaction that was admonished upon us by Andrew Carnegie.

And this is where I introduce you to the meaning of **Tron**:

An instrument/vessel

A Tron is any device that functions as a Window into Metadata.

Therefore, Metatron is "that which is beyond the vessel".

What does this mean?

If your phone, computer, smart watch, or I-Pad dies, your Metadata still lives!

This is mysterious and wonderful to contemplate, don't you think?

Yet, in the world of the Internet, there are people who do not have clear and authentic metadata (even Archbishop Harpazio Anastasis is purifying irrelevant and distracting Metadata at the time of the writing of this book).

In order to have authentic human interaction that bridges the world of the Internet with the offline world, your Metadata must become authentic.

You may be living two types of paths Online; the Royal Path and the Criminal path.

1. The Criminal Path is a crime against yourself that ends up being a crime against others.
2. The Royal Path is being true to yourself, which ends up you being true to others.

It's time for all of us to experience a profound repentance of our criminal Metadata!

That is, we must "think beyond" our criminal Metadata and become transformed.

The Royal Path is Metatron^{TM}

The Criminal Path is Spamatron^{TM}.

- Spamatron^{TM} is Metadata that seeks to interrupt, confuse, and distract Authentic Human Interaction.
- It actually isn't even true Metadata since that Metadata's purpose is Archival in Nature, to help humans find information much easier.
- In other words, Metadata is naturally humanitarian.

- Therefore, Spamatron™ and Spamadata are at War with Metatron™ and Metadata.
- Metatron Church™ is a Kingdom community of fellow Kings (Entrepreneurs), and those who want to serve Entrepreneurs, who have gathered themselves together to fight the Inner Spam within Ourselves.
- Inner and Outer Spam are entirely based on Wishful Thinking!
- Spamatron™ causes us to "hope", to secretly wish that our ideas will come to pass, and make us rich or famous or both.
- Spamatron™ is created from thinking "about" our problems, instead of thinking "beyond" our problems.
- Therefore, Metatron™ and Metatron Church™ are solution based!

Now it has been said by many successful and wealthy business folks that "Content is King."

But that could be the BIGGEST LIE of Spamatron™ yet!

<u>The truth is that Spamatron™ loves to give content.</u>

The problem is that this monster gives it at a time and place that no one wants!

Spamatron™ does not have a harmonious relationship to time and space

Spamatron™ provides content WHEN nobody wants it

Spamatron™ provides content HOW nobody wants it

Spamatron™ provides content WHERE nobody wants it

Spamatron™ provides content to WHO? The people who don't want it.

Spamatron™ provides WHAT? The wrong content.

Spamatron™ provides content WHY?

Because...

SPAMATRON™ IS A NEEDY PEASANT WHO DESPISES THE TRUE KINGS CALLED ENTREPRENEURS!

Content is NOT King.

ROYAL CONTENT IS KING[TM].

I'll happily repeat.

Content is NOT King.

ROYAL CONTENT IS KING[TM].

What makes content royal or noble?

It has to authentically relate to people.

The ancient astrologers created 12 Categories in the sky – Metadata - that represent The 12 Issues of Life[TM] , which are the very things that make us human.

What are The 12 Issues of Life[TM]?

Issue 1/Aries
Identity

Issue 2/Taurus
Finance

Issue 3/Gemini
Communication

Issue 4/Cancer
Home Life/Culture

Issue 5/Leo
Romance/love/children

Issue 6/Virgo
Work/service/health

Issue 7/Libra
Partnership

Issue 8/Scorpio
Sex/Transformation/Needs

Issue 9/Sagittarius
Marketing/Philosophy

Issue 10/Capricorn
Reputation/Career

Issue 11/Aquarius
Friendship/Society/Networking

Issue 12/Pisces
The Subconscious/Glamour/Hospitals/Prisons

You see, The 12 Issues of Life^{TM} are REAL.

But there is someone, something very FALSE; it is this Demon, this Monster called Spamatron^{TM}.

Spamatron^{TM} is unwilling to establish harmonious relationship to the 12 Issues of Humanity, and attempts to cause us to avoid these at all costs.

Spamatron^{TM} goes out of its way to create these 12 problems (falsities) for people:

12
Wants everyone else to be imprisoned, sick, and unaware like it

11
Doesn't seek to understand how society is linked

10
Could care less about its own reputation

9

Chooses the wrong audience for its message

8
Needy and never willing to improve itself

7
Lone ranger

6
Lazy

5
Wishful thinker

4
No principles that guide behavior

3
Doesn't acknowledge that there are two sides to a conversation

2
Cares not for providing value to the world

1
Has no sense of identity, and therefore your enemy, because would destroy your identity - if it could - in a heart beat

Spamatron™ is provided unjustified power by humans dehumanizing ourselves through continually "thinking about" our failures - the perverted definition of repentance given earlier.

<u>Instead of thinking about our failures let us fix our thoughts upon and about what our successes could be (the one part of The Law of Attraction film that actually works when combined with specific strategy for success).</u>

The antithesis to Spamatron™ thinking is...

The knowledge of The Royal Content Family™ = your Success Identity™

Metatron Church^{TM} is founded upon your Success Identity^{TM}

Success Identity^{TM} is how you choose to identity yourself to the world from an inner celebration of your Freedom of Thought (Metatron King), Freedom of Emotion (Metatron Queen), Freedom of Speech (Metatron Prince), and Freedom of Action (Metatron Princess).

So what is a Church of Success?

Church is from a Greek word, "Ecclesia" meaning "a called out gathering".

Metatron Church^{TM} is any gathering of people who unite themselves together in order to renounce association with Spamatron^{TM} and heed Archbishop Harpazio Anastasis's call to embrace The 12 Issues of Entrepreneurship^{TM} as their inspiration for Success, Gain, and Wealth.

The experience and explanation of Success, Gain, and Wealth in relation to The 12 Issues of Entrepreneurship^{TM} are what is meant by the Metatron Church^{TM} slogan, The Religion of Business^{SM}

What are the 12 Issues of Entrepreneurship^{TM} that Merlin Harpazio Anastasis so brilliantly brewed together into a Cauldron of Authentic Human Interaction?

Realize first that The 12 Issues of Entrepreneurship^{TM} are as UNAVOIDABLE as The 12 Issues of Life^{TM}.

Here is an Ultimate Philosophy for you to consider:

- The Universe which surrounds you at all times has been categorized into 12 types of Metadata.

- The theory is that the Zodiac Houses represent how we relate to the 12 Issues of Life, and therefore, how we relate to each other.

- How could we truly understand others if we don't understand ourselves?

- Nevertheless, even though these 12 Issues are Immortal, in that they will always be there, we can use our awareness of them to harmoniously manifest the type of life we want!

- This is proven by the simple comparison that the 12 musical notes are always there as a potential, but how we choose to play them is up to us.

The 12 Issues of Entrepreneurship™ that we must all embrace in order to avoid the influence and pitfalls of Spamatron™ are:

Issue 1/Aries
Metadata Identity

Issue 2/Taurus
Value of Products/Services

Issue 3/Gemini
Publicity/Social Media

Issue 4/Cancer
Company Culture

Issue 5/Leo
Passion – Love what you do/Do what you love

Issue 6/Virgo
Secret Operations/Practical Work

Issue 7/Libra
Alliances/Affiliates

Issue 8/Scorpio
Transformation/Evolution

Issue 9/Sagittarius
Marketing/True Audience

Issue 10/Capricorn
Status/Reputation

Issue 11/Aquarius
Networking

Issue 12/Pisces
Your Story

Let us consider for true moments of great contemplation the amazing power of what has been written so far.

For the very first time, that which has often been considered spiritual/metaphysical is accessible to anyone, anywhere, for the logical harnessing of ideas into material manifestation.

In consideration of the Great Power which has been bestowed upon you, let us turn to the symbol of The Dragon for Great Inspiration and Motivation.

In ancient Druidry, the Dragon was a symbol of Absolute Truth.

When you embrace the 12 Issues of Entrepreneurship^{TM} as the absolute universal essential elements of Success, Gain, and Wealth, you will have immediately harnessed the Dragon as your Pet.

Will the Dragon cease being a monster after harnessing its power?

Never!

But you will have great freedom to ride the dragon and inspire it to breathe fire at your beckoning [continue reading below to catch of glimpse of the fire you are about to claim as your own by virtue of training the Dragon Metatron^{TM} to be your pet].

Would you like to take advantage of aligning yourself to The Royal Content Family^{TM} to prepare yourself for battle against the inner and outer demons of Spamatron^{TM}?

It is time for you to embrace your Metadata Self^{TM} in the context of The Royal Content Family's Fiery Metatron King, Watery Metatron Queen, Airy Metatron Prince, and Earthy Metatron Princess.

Presented to you on the next page is an entirely fresh paradigm of Esoteric Spiritual Philosophy in the form of Intellectual Analysis, which you could immediately seize toward Material World Success.

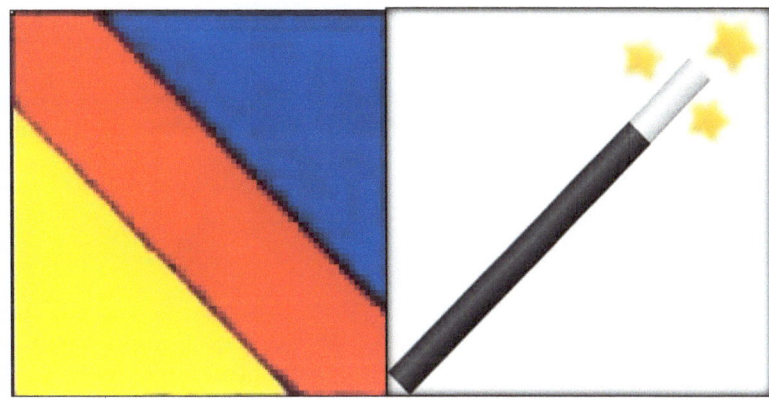

Align yourself to The Metatron King – Your Mission
(The 3 Powers of Merlin's Wand, Fire, and Your Sense of the Future)
Metadata Identity (Aries)
Your Passion (Leo)
Your Audience (Sagittarius)

Align yourself to The Metatron Queen – Your Motive
(3 Powers of Avalon's Cup, Water, and Your Sense of the Past)
Company Culture (Cancer)
Transformations (Scorpio)
Your Story (Pisces)

Align yourself to the Metatron Prince – Your Impact
(3 Powers of Excalibur, Air, and Your Sense of the Present)
Partnerships (Libra)
Networking (Aquarius)
Social Media/Publicity (Gemini)

Align yourself to The Metatron Princess – Your Legacy
(3 Powers of Camelot, Earth, and Your Sense of the Timeless)
Status/Reputation (Capricorn)
Value of Products/Services (Taurus)
Practical and Secret Work (Virgo)

In order to be baptized into our The Royal Content Family™ you must embrace the Dragon of the unavoidable Absolute Truths of Entrepreneurship, called Metatron™.

This is the image of Metatron™: The Dragon of Absolute Truth

When you have encountered and tamed the 12 Issues of Entrepreneurship™ within yourself, the Dragon who was once called Spamatron, will be transformed into a Metatron™.

Failure will become Success.

Loss will become gain.

Poverty will become wealth.

If you have established authentic Metadata on the Internet then you are technically already a Metatron™.

But in order to be officially regarded by us as Metatron Nobility™ you must go through our Katechism™ training as a Metatron Church™ Convert.

All Entrepreneurs have experienced Success Baptism™.

All Business Owners have experienced Profit Confirmation™.

All Enterprise Ventures have experienced Wealth Anointing™ (transfer of value through exponential sales growth, investment, or business acquisition).

If you currently are Successful, Profitable, or Wealthy you are an honorary member of The Royal Content Family™.

Yet there are 6 Technical Gates into Metatron Church™ that are only entered through the possession of 6 Keys called "Clergy Vestments":

Success Baptism
Profit Confirmation
Wealth Anointing
Parishioner
Convert
Metatron Nobility (those who apply their Katechism™ training)

Those who have utilized their 6 Clergy Vestments are worthy to be publically supported and acknowledged as Clergy of Metatron Church™.

All of the basic organizational structures of "The Church" are covered fully in Katechism™.

All that being said you are invited to become a Parishioner (sojourner) in our midst, and you truly are since you've been reading this book.

By continuing to sojourn with us and explore our truths you could monumentally impact society, and quite possibly earn yourself more clarity in your life, for associates, and your old/new ventures.

Go to www.metatronchurch.biz and invest your time and resources into **The Camelot** of our **Square X Factor Society**™.

Archbishop Harpazio Anastasis is the pen name for musician Harpazio. He has magically combined his own unique Philosophy of Entrepreneurship (sometimes referring to it as The Religion of Business), with his songwriting career. He maintains that music is the best tool to communicate ideas simply; a more efficient means than information based books like this. He has invested great care into structuring lyrical music albums accompanied by reasonably short companion books.

The 1st short book is from his album, "I Am The Phoenix", structured to inspire anyone out of failure, loss, and poverty. By seeing yourself as your own Legendary Phoenix Bird you could confidently fail, lose, and become poor with the expectation that you will always Rise from the Ashes. "You Are the Phoenix" is the prequel to the Bishop's forthcoming book, "Every Entrepreneur Is a King" which heralds the onset and mission of Metatron

Church^{TM}, the full embodiment of The Archbishop's "Religion of Business". The 1st is motivational, assisting the emotional transformation needs of anyone seeking to awaken their dreams into reality. The 2nd is inspirational and provides specific practical solutions to combating inner and outer enemies that conspire to fate a person to a life of Peasantry.

A related book to both (targeted primarily at musicians) is called, "Why Most Starving Artists Deserve to be Poor: Feed the Elephant in the Room." That book is unique for him in that it has no companion album and is also the foundation behind an interdependent record label concept he calls K.N.O.W.N. Enterprises^{TM}.

_____

Ventures of The Bishop in either concept or operational phases:

Concept:

www.metatronchurch.biz

www.knownenterprises.com

www.harpazio.knownenterprises.com

Operational:

www.keyidentityaccess.com
(piano learning curriculum that teaches beginners to write their own songs)
_____

Lyrical Albums of The Bishop:

https://soundcloud.com/harpazio-music/sets/i-am-the-phoenix